A Graphic Approach to Creativity

Also by Michele Cassou

BOOKS

- **Life, Paint and Passion:** Reclaiming the Magic of Spontaneous Expression
- **Point Zero:** Creativity Without Limits
- **Kids Play:** Igniting Children's Creativity
- **The Buddhist Art Doctor:** Prescriptions for Creative and Non-Creative Seekers
- **Teachers That Dare:** Using the Creative Process to Teach the Creative Process
- **Answering the Call of Creativity**
- **Questions:** To Awaken Your Creative Power to the Fullest

DVDs and Vimeo Downloads
Awakening of the Mystic
Birth of a Process
Point Zero: Insights and Images
The Flowering of Children's Creativity
Body, Sexuality and Spirit
Morning Talks on Creativity
The Forgotten Secrets of Creativity

www.michelecassou.com
CICF (nonprofit): cassou-institute.com
Email: cassouinstitute@gmail.com

A Graphic Approach to Creativity

INTUITIVE CREATIVITY MADE SIMPLE

Michele Cassou

ISBN: 197757839X
ISBN 13: 9781977578396

Contents

This book...

THERE IS A GREAT DEPTH of inspiration that blooms when intuition and creativity work together. In this book, I will use graphics designed to reveal creativity's natural principles, its obstacles, and the anatomy of creative blocks. The graphics also expose the true and often surprising nature of intuition, bringing a profound understanding that can overcome the roots of creative problems.

This book is a powerful and easy-to-use tool to stimulate authentic inspiration and to show in a unique way the essence of creativity and its amazing principles.

About the Birth of this Little Book

WHEN I WAS LEADING CREATIVITY training sessions, I become so passionate about conveying the deepest understanding of creativity to my students that one day, I drew a diagram to show my point—and then, I kept drawing. These little scribbles were a success because they allowed *instant understanding* of the basic principles of creativity. I enjoyed so much their clarity and power of communication that I drew more and more of them, to the delight of my students. To my great surprise, they felt it helped them a lot to understand how creativity works. Soon, I decided to put these drawings in a little book to inspire and teach those searching for a deeper understanding of the great gift of creativity. Here it is to enjoy!

Who Paints What?

Two Ways to Approach Creativity

1. **Through pure intuition**

   When we listen to intuition, the entire being, heart, and soul respond and create, using the energy of life with all its layers. Intuition paints what is needed and obvious in the moment, always responding *spontaneously* to the present state and the intelligence of *Being*. The painter paints what is ripe and ready -- not what is wanted! Intuitive creation is a harmonious response from the whole.

2. **Through learning, control, and choices**

   When we respond to the traditional rules and aesthetics of cultural customs, trying to reproduce a theme or subject that we have imagined or chosen, the intellect dictates the work. The image of the expected product is planed and limited by preferences, aesthetics, meaning, or tradition, so pure and free creativity becomes impossible.

The River of Creativity

A Clear Look at the Creative Flow

The flow of creativity is the core of the flow of life and passes through all there is; in us it is a constant stream of life energy.

The beds of the river of life amass deposits. Deposits are made out of repressed or denied emotional or mental materials that float in the stream. These deposits accumulate on the riverbanks, narrowing the natural flow of creativity. These deposits in time become *creative blocks*, obstructing the natural path to creative energy.

These deposits are built from fears, wounds, prejudices, expectations, desire for product, or just anything wanted, unfinished, denied, or repressed; or they could be simply made up of traditional rules. In time, they become rigid and grow larger narrowing the flows of creativity; they can even block the current fully for many years.

Confronting the creative blocks

In creativity, we learn to go around or destroy the deposits and the blocks by listening to intuition. Intuitive creativity spontaneously aims at the deposits, then cracks and destroys them, freeing the current.

Loops are the result of the temptation to escape the blocks by settling safely in a small, and fixed place. Loops can be comfortable—but are often boring and stagnant.

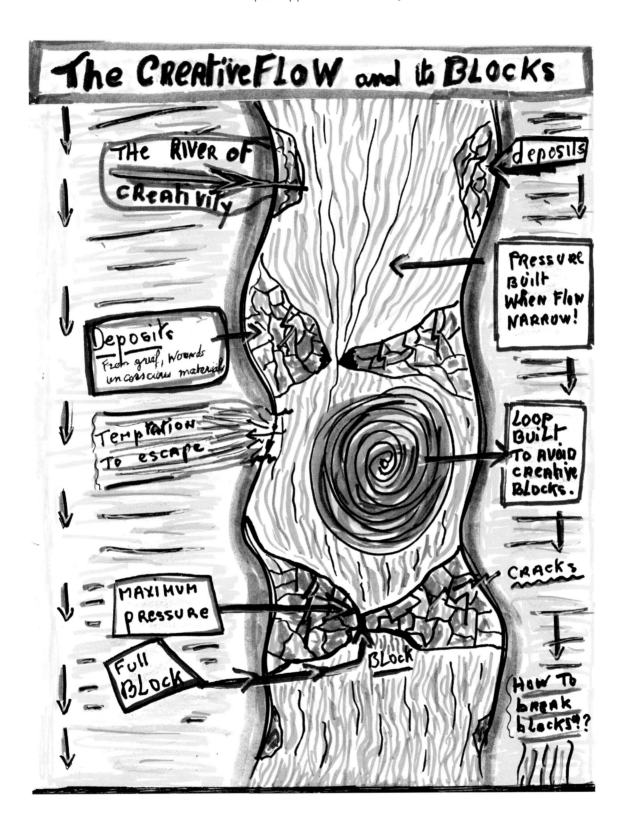

The Wisdom of Creativity

Intuition versus Mental Choices

The graphic shows that the entire sum of our conscious and unconscious life is constantly in present time—action- reaction, action-reaction—never stopping. Thousands of impressions, perceptions, and feelings are present at every moment, most of them usually ignored or repressed or simply unnoticed.

In the drawing, you can see the lines of your lived life reaching the present. Pure intuition does not ignore them. *It responds to the whole spectrum of feelings in the present*, not just what had been selected or desired by imagination. Intuition always responds to and expresses all past experiences and perceptions, conscious and unconscious, we call it the exploration of the unknown.

Choosing a special subject to create, on the other hand, makes you abandon the richness of the present and the unexpected and make you control the work according to expectations, conditioning, and learned preferences.

Ponder on the amazing limitations of mental choices and their consequences, disguised as freedom.

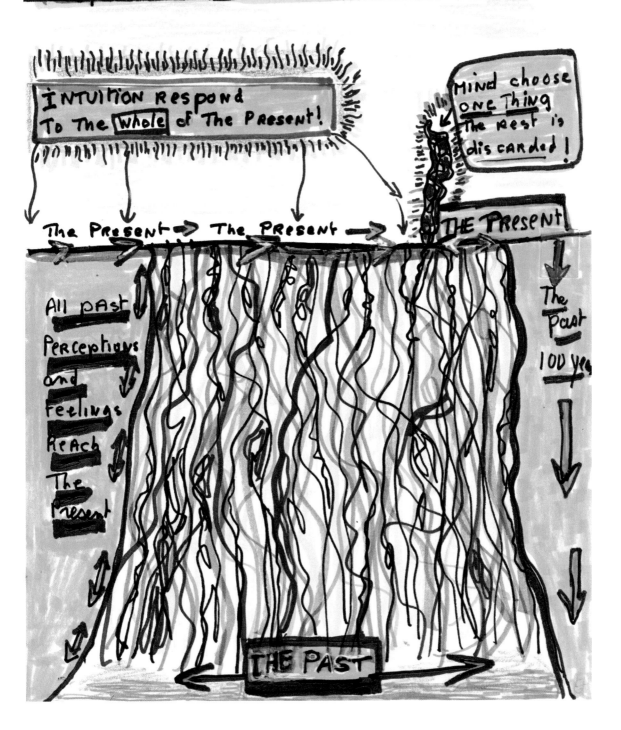

The Natural Gravity of Creativity

Stored Emotions and Repressed Materials Move Into the Present like
Bubble In a Glass
when we are Free and Spontaneous.
This is a Natural Principle.

In intuitive creativity, pockets of stored old or new experiences, memories and perceptions empty themselves naturally, if there are no controlling interference or blocks in their way.

When kept prisoners by expectations and prejudices, the bubbles can't help but stay frozen and buried. When freed by intuition, they reach the vast spaces of freedom of expression, disintegrate, and dissolve into unlimited space, bringing wisdom.

Realize how important it is for a creative person to get rid of his or her limiting preferences and get out of the way for creative gravity to do its harmonizing work.

Control and will are the main barriers to true intuitive creativity. Discover on how dramatically important it is to understand how creativity works in order to reach the fullness of expression, which can only be propelled by inner intuitive freedom.

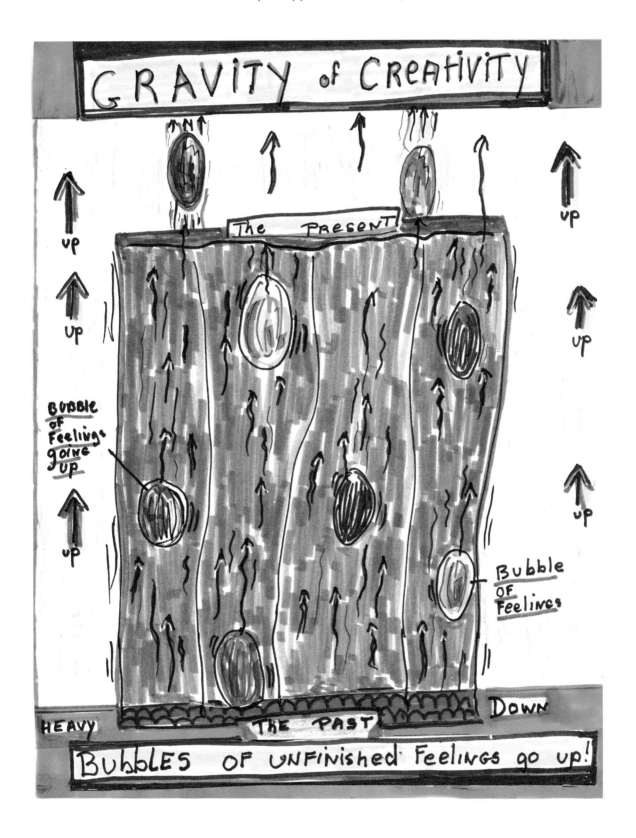

The Unknown at Work

POCKETS OF MIND WITH THEIR TIES

Unconscious pockets of repressed emotional materials are *tied with knots,* originally to prevent suffering. These pockets are filled with past events, grief, wounds, repressed feelings, or anything unfinished or unresolved or simply pushed away from consciousness.

When intuition explores the unknown, it spontaneously *opens the pocket's ties* to allow repressed feelings to fly out and resolve themselves.

When the ties are open, the contents of the pockets are finally set free and instinctively move up like bubbles.

Let's remember that intuition works incessantly at emptying the filled pockets. When the repressed contents escape, they fulfill their purposes through expression and, then dissolve when they enter the present.

Intuitive creativity unloads the burden of the unfinished past, clears it up, and brings harmony and healing to consciousness.

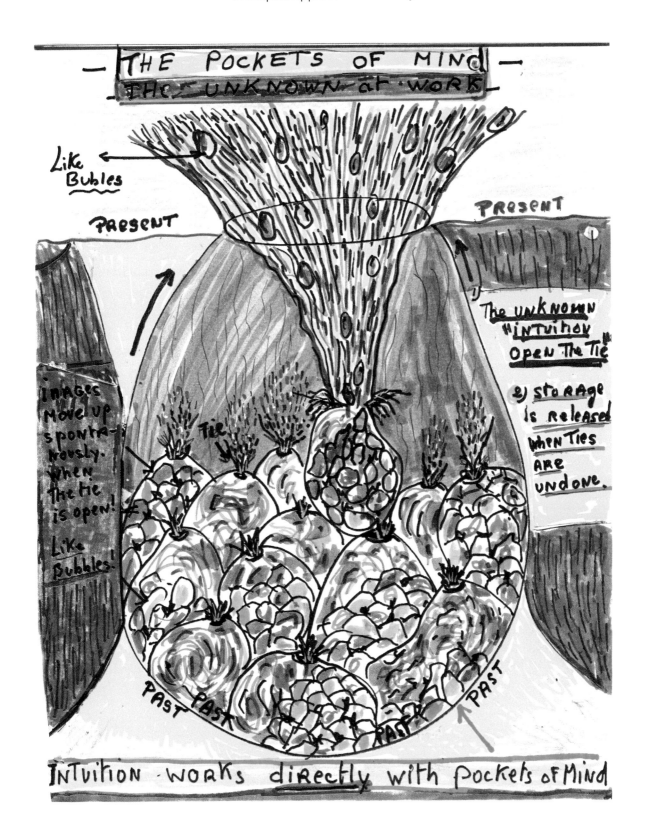

Illumination on the Power of Completion

COMPLETION IS A MAGIC KEY THAT OPENS THE SECRETS OF THE SOUL.

Completion of the creative work is reached by challenging the mind to get out of the way and by being willing to explore the unknown, the different, and the unfamiliar.

How to stimulate deep intuition when finishing a creative work:
* Ask impossible questions
* Cross borders
* Jump into the unknown
* Dare, risk, experiment
* Break taboos
* Let yourself truly feel anything

Powerful effects of completion:
* Stimulates and make you transcends levels of Being
* Spontaneously explores the roots of feelings
* Awakens hidden senses and stimulates healing
* Brings ever-new discoveries and their wisdom
* Leads to the narrow door of the unknown and its mystery
* Fulfills creativity by stimulating its power of intuition

For instance, enter deeper layers of your work by asking yourself the following questions:

What could come out of a very precise place in your work?
What would I do if I were not afraid to go too far? To be too strange?

The Questioning Spoon

MOVING THE CREATIVE POTENTIAL AND ITS ENERGY

The stirring of a daring spoon breaks down routine,
habits, conditioning, and especially expectations.
It fires up the inspiration to create.
The spoon's work is often revealed by the finishing work.

Spontaneous sharp questions can be used like a spoon stirring a big pot of settled materials—rules, beliefs, expectations, repressions, and desires for results.

The questioning spoon, with its intense action, brings back the movement of spontaneity to creation and unearths a world of possibilities and dimensions. The stirring brings the unexpected out of its hidden places and up to the surface, allowing pure expression in the moment, in the being and allowing authenticity.

After a while of this intense stirring activity, the spoon cracks the container of stored mental and emotional materials. Once the container is broken spontaneity is free to move about, expand, create and surprise you.

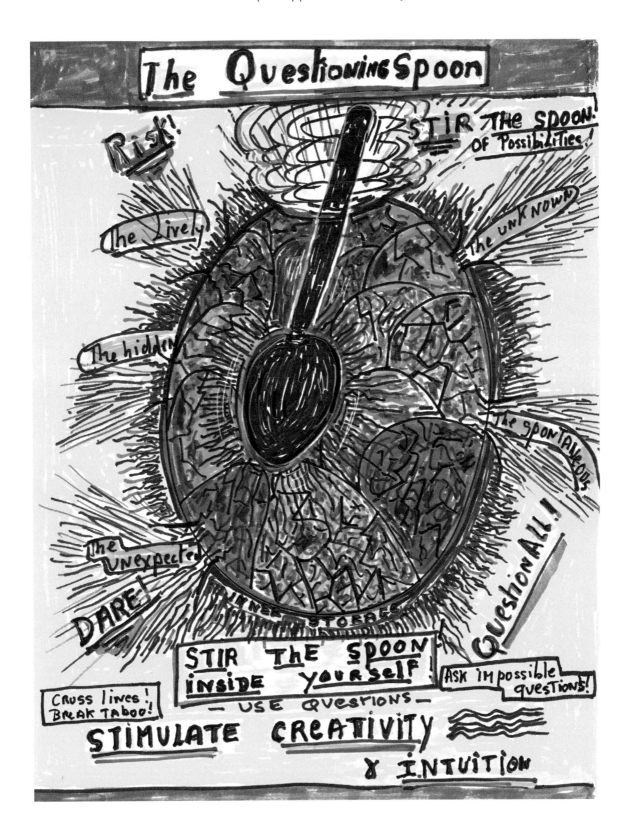

Big Images and Their Potential

DEVELOP THE ART OF USING WHAT YOU HAVE ALREADY DONE TO JUMP INTO THE MYSTERIOUS UNKNOWN.

Never be stopped or intimidated by what you have done, even when it is a very large image, almost filling the whole page. On the contrary, use it as a starting point to explore beyond and to open the inner screen. Always challenge the expected future and the space your creation is occupying. A big wide world is surrounding your work on many layers and dimensions, look at it, imagine a huge white empty space around it and let yourself wander in it.

Let creativity know that *you* know that all the cards have not been played yet. The mystery can still enter, and there might be a lot more to discover even when a big image has appeared.

A surprise is often waiting around, anxious to be revealed to your consciousness. Even another big image can appear, or just a part of one.

The Mousetrap: Going for the Cheese!

GOING FOR PROCESS—NOT PRODUCT!
HAVING A SET PLAN OR BEING FREE?

"Going for the cheese!" illustrates going for the result you have in mind, for what is known, planned, expected or wanted.

If you already know what you're after, the result is already set. **If you want cheese, you will get cheese. Period.**

The door of the new and lively is closed; the unfamiliar won't enter your work, won't surprise you, won't make you truly explore. The depth and the surprise will stay away. Your path is already written. Your creativity has landed in a small place, caught in a trap!

Watch what happens inside you when you "go for the cheese."

* Intuition has no place to explore the mystery of who you are on any level.
* You have escaped the reality of the present and are creating in a stereo-typical secondhand world.

Ask yourself, "Is this cheese what I really want?"

Expanding the Field of Creation

BECOMING AWARE OF THE WIDE FIELD BEYOND THE PERSONAL STORAGE WAREHOUSE.

The following illustration points at the space around you. That space is there at all times and around everything you create: it is unlimited, full of endless potential. You must become curious and adventurous and listen to the subtle demands of wild inspiration.

When you create from intuition, you learn to challenge and probe *the boundaries of the known from the inside and from the outside*; always being certain that there is more to discover beyond your familiar consciousness. You can scan beyond what you can imagine, for instance, by asking, "What could be a thousand miles away?" or "What could be hiding very close by?" –you can invent all kinds of questions challenging the borders of time and space.

You can ask to go beyond the limits of the imaginable and plunge right into the mystery of life and spirit (outside, beyond, beyond the beyond, underneath, down, up, through, etc.). When you keep exploring outside the known into the vast space and great mystery around you, your open attitude and courageous spirit attract new perceptions of life. You will become amazed and delighted at what can appear, all of a sudden, out of you and out of the infinite mystery of life.

The Strategy of Interpretation

UNDERSTOOD INTERPRETATION OFFERS
SPONTANEOUS INSIGHTS

Traditional interpretation most often encloses the creative work in what is already known, guessed, or deducted on one level of consciousness only.

In that way, interpretation *builds fences* against the truly new and unexpected. Interpretation stays on the *same dimension* as the level of inquiry.

To interpret a creative work is like setting a major stop sign for genuine discoveries; it freezes what has happened and what is already known. It often gives seductive reasons for staying in the narrow space of projections and expectations. It also often tricks with flattery, control or even mockery to resolve the desired issues.

Let's remember that beyond interpretation, there is the great unknown, the infinite mystery of life, the unending unexpected that comes from behind the screen of thoughts and is propelled out by intuition. Its wonderful and wise gifts are **insights and revelations**. (With interpretation, however, insights have no place to arise.)

The Fifth Dimensional Dot

*THE ONE DETAIL THAT GOES BEYOND
AND CHANGES EVERYTHING*

Introducing <u>sharp focus</u> inside your inner world.
Intuition, when *keenly* listened to, guides you to see beyond superficial levels of reality into greater depths and states of Being. You, as a creator become a pioneer, you explore *other dimensions* and you become aware of a mysterious universe.

When traveling the hidden world, the unknown, the unperceived beyond your momentary consciousness, you find a most wonderful, surprising, and passionate experience.

Intuition can focus like a laser to crack the layers that are blocking deeper dimensions. You need to let intuition *focus on every last small dot or mark* to penetrate any possible space into what is beyond. It is similar to a magic key that opens inner doors.

At that point, the full completion with its small magical dots leads you to new inner roads, to new levels, and exposes secrets from beyond the visible world.

When you enter these faraway spaces, the intelligence of the universe opens your senses and your seeing, while guiding you endlessly through the discovery of the unknown.

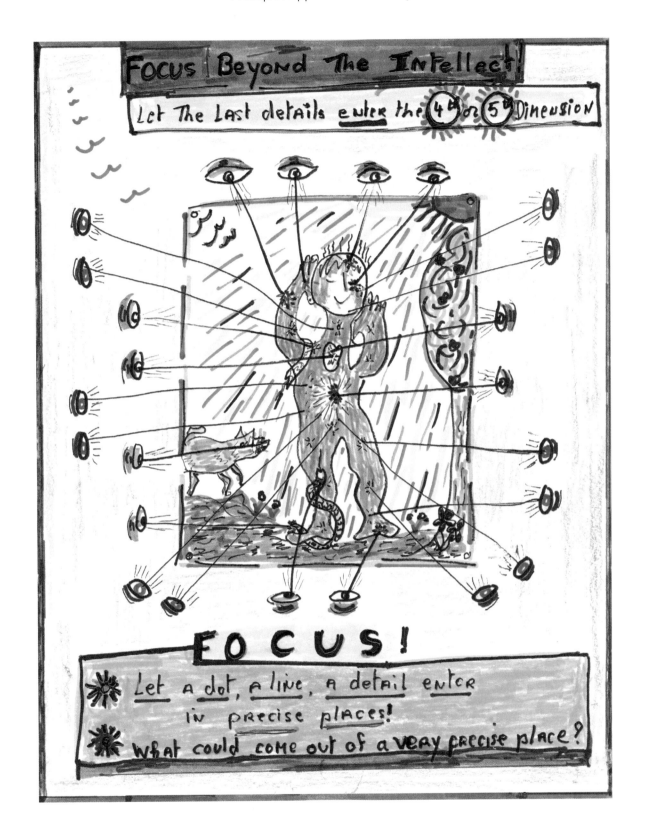

Deconstructing the Ego

Breaking the Boundaries of Self-Definition

Discover how creative intuition shatters the boundaries of ego that were built, reinforced, and expanded along the many years.

The ego container slowly breaks due to the movement and activity generated inside its territory by intuitive creativity. The energy of intuition always needs more space to move, expand, discover.

During intuitive creation, the boundaries of the known *weaken more and more* and finally crack, as other dimensions and feelings are revealed. Spontaneously, the energy of exploration explodes the former limits of the ego and is on its way out to encounter amazing discoveries.

Surprises, laughter, and well-being arise outside the borders, because what is fully new, unexpected, and outside the conditioned routine carries joy, fulfillment, insights, and healing.

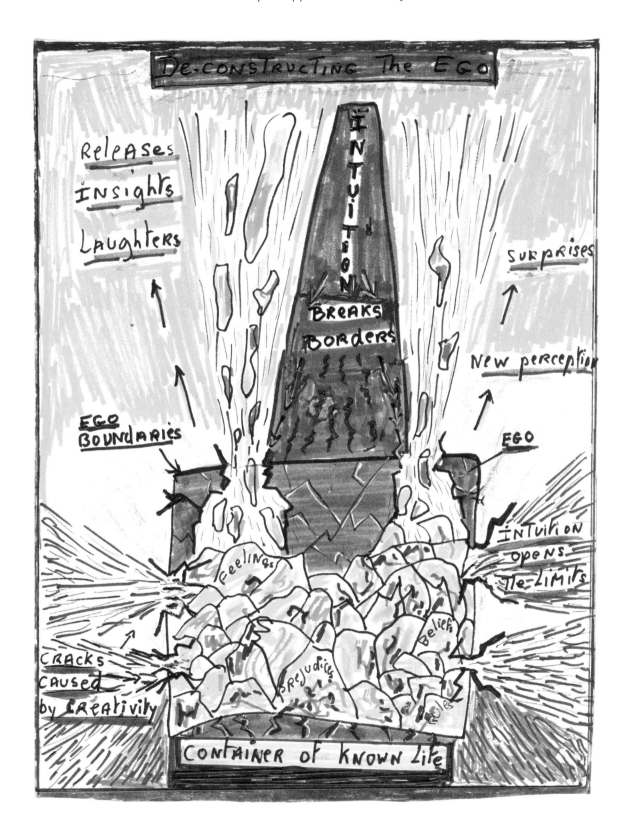

MICHELE CASSOU, A PASSIONATE PAINTER and teacher, is the founder of an original method of creative painting. She was born and raised in southern France. As a young adult, she moved to Paris, where she studied law, literature, and art. Inspired by watching children paint, she discovered a way to express herself spontaneously and without the need for conventional training. A unique approach to creativity grew out of her many years of "just painting for herself."

She is known internationally for her groundbreaking work in freeing the creative potential and exploring the spiritual dimensions of the creative process. She has taught thousands of students for more than four decades. She currently conducts workshops in the San Francisco area; at the Esalen Institute in Big Sur, California; and at the Mabel Dodge Luhan house in Taos, New Mexico. She also gives web courses.

A passionate artist, she has painted thousands paintings, authored many books, and produced videos and CDs of her work. Though educated in Paris, she has lived most of her life in California, where she continues to paint and write, teach and train. In 2016, she founded with a board a nonprofit organization, CIFC, which offers outreach programs to needy communities.

ACKNOWLEDGMENTS

I WANT TO GIVE MY heartfelt thanks to those who have been on my road, committed and interested in this marvelous creative process. They have stimulated and inspired my teaching discoveries. Students and student-teachers have motivated me to keep searching in new and deeper ways how to teach creativity and convey the great power and possibilities it offers.

I am grateful to all those who supported me along the path, with heartfelt thanks to Jana Zanetto and Philippe Tenenhaus for their invaluable help in editing the manuscript, with particular warm thanks to Cherie Ray, Anna Billings, Gwinn Lowman, and Jane Malek, who were fully open and committed to learn to become the best teachers they could be.

The nonprofit board CICF was also a great motivating inspiration for me with Stuart Piontek, Linda Applewhite, Jo-René Roseberry, and Bonnie Cohen.

Thanks to these wonderful friends that offered care and love during the making of this book and who continue to work to make this amazing process go on in the future.

Made in the USA
Middletown, DE
11 March 2020